# SACRED PEARLS

# SACRED PEARLS

## Pearl

ARTHUR H. STOCKWELL LTD
Torrs Park   Ilfracombe   Devon
*Established 1898*
*www.ahstockwell.co.uk*

*British Library Cataloguing-in-Publication Data.*
*A catalogue record for this book is available*
*from the British Library.*

ISBN 978-0-7223-4011-0
*Printed in Great Britain by*
*Arthur H. Stockwell Ltd*
*Torrs Park   Ilfracombe*
*Devon*

# 1

Lord, let us stop and pray awhile
On our journey to the sky.
We have come from far-off Earth,
Where we witnessed Jesus' birth.

Our Queen of Heaven is with you now,
And we have fondly come to bow.
Radiantly crowned upon her throne,
Her open arms to welcome home.

Lord, let us stop and pray awhile
On our journey to the sky.
All the saints on bended knee,
All are there to be with Thee.

Grant us, O Lord, a place in Heaven,
Now our sins have been forgiven.
We have rested for a while,
Now let us see Our Lady's smile.

# 2

Thank You for the sun.
Thank You for the rain.
Thank You for our Heaven,
Where You alone do reign.

We should count our blessings.
We have You in our world
And our Blessed Lady
Who keeps us safe, we are told.

Guardian angels one by one
Are standing on the stairs
To show the way to Heaven –
To One we know who cares.

Lord, let us in Your garden
To find eternal peace.
We will close our eyes for ever,
But joy will never cease.

# 3

O, holy sweet mother of Our Lord,
How very much you are adored!
Your radiant face and beaming smile –
Please teach us how to pray awhile.

Your Son is with us day and night,
And makes the angels shine so bright.
O, Blessed Mother crowned above,
How we know of your sweet love!

Upon the Cross our dear Lord died,
With His sweet mother by His side.
The forgiveness still within His heart –
A prayer to His Father to let them depart.

We will all go to Heaven
At the end of our day.
Our Father is waiting,
So now we must pray.

# 4

Is it love that's in the garden?
There's beauty all around.
It's the things that God created
That's making all the sound.

The trees we see, the flowers we smell,
Are sent from Heaven above,
And all the little creatures
Were made so well with love.

There's lady's smocks and maidenhair –
Each little petal created with care.
God made us all with tender love –
The sun, the moon, the Heaven above.

So take a walk in the garden,
And take in all that's around.
There's lots of love in the garden,
And God will soon be found.

# 5

What's this meaning of paradise,
Somewhere beyond our control?
It's where we are loved for ever,
And where things are best left untold.

We've wiped the slate clean with our conscience,
And our penance we've left behind.
We are on our way to Heaven,
To the One that we know is kind.

It's been a long, long journey,
But now the time has come
To fly off to Heaven for ever
And to share our dear Lord's home.

Familiar faces are at the gates –
I am sure they will let me in.
I am on my way to Heaven
To hear the angels sing.

## 6

The mountain mist is rising
As I gaze across the sea,
Knowing you are always there
And over here is me.

I pray a little more each day
For God to keep you safe,
As you are teaching all of those
To have a little faith.

And over here we have faith too –
It's taught us every day –
And blessings abundant everywhere
To help us on our way.

So distance is no object.
No matter where we are,
We hold our hearts and close our eyes
And God will soon be there.

# 7

The room was bare except for the Cross,
But it was all I needed after my loss –
The floorboards hard against my knees,
And just the sound of wind in the trees.

It was the day after I buried my love,
And of course I knew he was up above.
He was in a garden somewhere in Heaven
After asking God to be forgiven.

The angels had come and took him away
For he was very tired that day.
Our Lord had called him home to rest –
And, after all, He does know best.

So as I kneel at the Cross and pray,
He comes with the Lord to see me each day.
So the pain in my knees is well worth while,
For every day I am left with a smile.

# 8

The children playing in the street,
The cobbles sore beneath their feet,
Their tattered clothes seen better a day
And the little things don't know how to pray.

They don't know a lady is up above,
Watching over them with tender love.
One day she will see a smile on their face
When they learn of God's good grace.

The children woke under the stars one morn,
And were happy for once about the dawn.
They have heard a lady has been to town,
And when she was seen she was wearing a crown.

She said if we prayed upon our knees,
And went to our shelter under the trees,
The angel would come and keep us warm
And God will make sure we come to no harm.

# 9

As I gaze towards the west,
It will be the place I want to rest.
There's peace and love within the sky,
And when we go we don't really die.

A little faith is what we need,
And take with us our good prayer beads.
We can join the angels and sing a song,
And I am sure with the saints we will get along.

Our Holy Mother is ready for us,
So let's just go without a fuss.
Our Lord is waiting to take in all,
And we will know when we get His call.

Happy are those who rest in peace,
Where our lives will never cease,
A mantle round us day and night,
And always the star that shines so bright.

# 10

As I gaze at the stars with love,
My heart rejoices at what's up above.
I can hear a song in a distant land
And see the shape of a very dear hand.

It's saying, "We are happy here in Heaven,
And this is our home after being forgiven."
Some were not happy on this earth;
They've been waiting for God since the day of their birth.

So go down on your knees at the Cross and pray,
And ask the Lord to have you some day.
Promise to be good when up above,
And open your arms to his tender love.

And if you are happy on this earth now,
Just think of Our Lady and take a bow.
One day you'll be praying on bended knee,
For her great love above you'll see.

# 11

A prayer or two is what we need,
And we don't always have to read.
Just close your eyes and thank the Lord,
And think of nothing else but good.

We can teach ourselves just what to say,
And we will learn just how to pray.
A few prayer beads will help us too,
And don't forget He always hears you.

You can always pray wherever you are,
And especially gazing at a star.
Beside your bed is good to kneel –
At the foot of a cross you will get the feel.

So let's all try once on our knees,
And don't forget you have to say *please*.
Our Lord will answer when He can,
And He will be kind to every man.

# 12

If I ever need someone,
I close my eyes and You will come
Like a dream in the night,
But O, so gentle with power and might.

No one can see You, but Your presence is felt,
And You are here so quickly I've not even knelt.
Please tell me again what's in Your world.
We will be there one day, the angels have told.

So thank You for coming; I knew that You would.
To see You once! If only I could!
I will tell my friends You are always near.
And we know it's for all that You really care.

# 13

The clouds are white and fluffy,
Passing across the sky.
It's what I hope is beyond them
That really makes me cry.

I weep for joy now I have found You.
I've tried to heal my aching heart.
I don't know how ever I left You,
Or why we were apart.

I really ask forgiveness
And will never leave You again –
Or Our Blessed Lady,
Whom I very much retain.

So please let's all renew our faith
And we will start again
To hold You very dear to us
While You above do reign.

# 14

As I pray at the Cross and weep,
There's no such thing as going to sleep.
The night has come and nearly gone,
And still I think I am here alone.

I thought my faith was strong to know
That You do really love us so.
I weep for Your pain and not my sin;
With the ache in my heart I will let You in.

I really know You are here all day,
And always hear me when I pray.
I look at Your Cross with tender love,
And weep with joy that You are up above.

So it's best not to weep, but rejoice in our heart,
For clearly Our Lord will never depart.
So smile at the Cross and feel Him near,
And above all remember that He really does care.

# 15

Love thy neighbour is what we teach,
But often we find them out of reach.
We try to teach them a little prayer,
But they are suspicious if they think we care.

They have no greater friend than our dear Queen,
But they won't believe what they haven't seen.
So we tell how she watches us and prays,
And hope they'll feel God one of these days.

You can only be a friend kind and true,
And hope one day they will ask you
To teach them faith and how to pray
And ask Our Dear Lord to visit some day.

It would take from them a lot of pain,
And make them see life is good again,
To see them smile when they see a cross;
And then you will know all is not lost.

# 16

Our Lady is sleeping and hears a cry –
It's a little Baby come down from the sky.
His little smile is so loving too,
And already He's happy to be here with you.

The Wise Men came from afar to see
Sweet little Jesus a-praying for me.
He was off to the temple to pray to the Lord,
His Mother surprised that He knew the word.

The time had come to see the world,
But He'd need some help for His word to be told.
So fishermen, doctors and collectors too
Would follow him dearly and preach to you.

He mended and healed and gave them life,
And the people around He'd unburden their strife.
It didn't last long – real pain had to come,
And they caught Him one night in a garden near home.

# 17

High on a hill was a Man on the Cross –
It will always be our greatest loss.
The nails in His feet and the sword in His side –
It was really for us Our Dear Lord died.

He died so He could be our Friend,
So His dear Father His body did mend.
And now we sing praise that He is near,
For He is the greatest Man who ever did care.

We go to the temple to ask for His love,
And He reassures us we will sing up above.
So let's close our eyes and give Him praise –
It was with such love we saw Him raise.

He will always be near us, we must believe,
And I am sure in Heaven we will be received.
So let's all enjoy His praise while we can,
And at the end of our prayers we will say amen.

# 18

Now you have all learnt to pray,
Your rosary beads will help you say
Our Lord's Prayer – it's a very good start,
And ten Hail Marys where the beads are apart.

So kiss the Cross and let's begin –
Your right hand, of course, it has to be in.
Our Holy Mother is waiting to hear
All our little rosary prayers.

We teach our little children to say
Three Hail Marys when they begin to pray,
So when they grow big and count to ten
They will achieve the goal up until the amen.

So close your eyes and feel the beads,
And you will find mysteries when you feel the need.
Our Lord will help, so take your time
And when you've learnt all you will feel divine.

# 19

When you have a very bad day,
It will be the time to really pray.
You will feel a good deal more content,
But your prayers must also be really meant.

Just ask Him for His peace and love,
And He will hear you from above.
And then His presence you will feel,
Because it will always help you heal.

So now that you are feeling fine
Just thank Him for being so divine.
So once again just close your eyes
And how great you feel you will be surprised.

So don't forget just what to do
When you are feeling very blue.
Just clasp your hands and think of good,
And see how it really changes your mood.

# 20

The end of the day is drawing near,
So we say our prayers with those who care.
A happy, long day we have had;
Now it's time for us to rejoice and be glad.

The little children are fast asleep,
And we ask Jesus for just a peep.
He'll keep them safe till morning's nigh;
Then with a stretch you'll hear a sigh.

If waking up is hard to do,
Ask an angel to come and help you.
Once you hear her tender song,
It will help you really get along.

So now we know that God has been,
And He is here for ever, though rarely seen.
So let's just get on with our day,
And He will be with us at rest and play.

# 21

My favourite cross is tall and wide,
And has an angel by its side.
His head is bowed in reverent prayer;
He is praying to God with every care.

His prayers are asking for peace and love
For a very dear friend who has joined Him above.
It was a bit too soon and sad,
For he was only a little lad.

The angels wanted him to play –
They would have such fun each and every day.
They would tuck him up at night,
And leave on the light that shines so bright.

So weep no more, for he is safe
And getting lots of God's good grace.
And all the angels are watching him,
And with little children there is no sin.

# 22

As I go back to the church in the hills –
It's where I found peace and love.
And if you look at the rooftop tall,
There might still be a dove.

An olive branch we have to show
When we have wronged our friends,
And I am sure we will have some help
When making our amends.

*Sorry* is a special word –
It's sometimes hard to say,
But I am sure, with hand on heart,
We can say it when we pray.

It will make you feel much better,
Asking to be forgiven
If you have wronged a very true friend
While on your way to Heaven.

# 23

As I look across the sea and smile,
I know You are with us, every wave, every mile.
So the sea is not as cruel as some think –
You walked on water and did not sink.

Your presence is felt every inch of the way,
Whether we go by night or by day.
Across the sea I am going for love,
While You are watching from above.

And when I get there I will pray
In a chapel without delay.
I will find one that is tall and wide
And has a cross right by its side.

Thank You, God, for keeping with me,
And now an angel I must see.
I will listen to his heart of gold
And hear the stories always told.

## 24

Let us rejoice in the Lord,
And praise Him still with loud applaud.
It's the start of a very good prayer,
Sharing all of God's very good care.

He has sent someone to watch and pray,
And keep us safe each and every day,
So let's clasp our hands and thank the Lord
For thinking of us as only good.

We will say a prayer to our dear Queen,
And tell her of the things we've seen.
We can hear the angels singing above,
As she watches us with tender love.

So we will meet with our friends to pray,
And God will come to us without delay.
He will tell us how to spread His love
While He is watching from above.

# FAREWELL TO ANTRIM

There's faith in the mountains and love all around,
And beauty beyond compare.
To find a cross word between any friends
Is ever so ever so rare.

Our Lady's mantle is around each home
And showing them how she cares –
The little children tucked up in bed
After saying all their prayers.

God's creatures are living off the earth –
The grass is very green,
And you only know the sun's been out
When a rainbow you have seen.

I wouldn't change it for the world.
It's the place I long to be.
So I'll go off with an aching heart,
But I will come right back to your sea.